SAMBURU

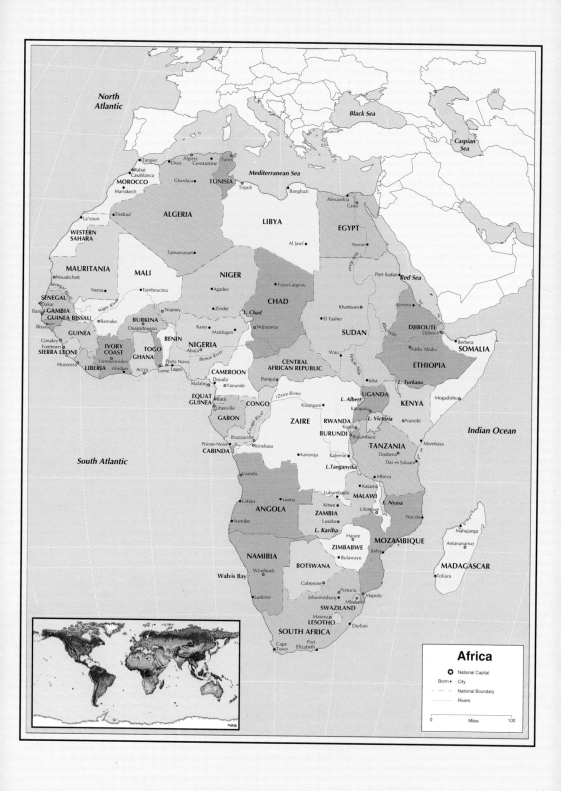

North
Atlantic

Black Sea

Caspian
Sea

Mediterranean Sea

Tangier
Oran Algiers Constantine Tunis
Rabat
Casablanca
MOROCCO Ghardaia **TUNISIA** Tripoli Banghazi
Marrakech Alexandria Cairo
ALGERIA **LIBYA** **EGYPT**
La'youn Tindouf Al Jawf Aswan
**WESTERN
SAHARA**
Tamanrasset
MAURITANIA Port Sudan **Red Sea**
Nouakchott **MALI** **NIGER** Faya-Largeau
Nema Agadez **CHAD** Khartoum Asmera
Tombouctou Zinder El Fasher **DJIBOUTI**
SENEGAL Niamey L. Chad Ndjamena Djibouti
Dakar Kano Maiduguri **SUDAN** Berbera
Bamako **BURKINA** Wau Addis Ababa
GAMBIA Ouagadougou Abuja **SOMALIA**
GUINEA BISSAU **BENIN** **ETHIOPIA**
Bissau **GUINEA** **NIGERIA** **CENTRAL** L. Turkana
Conakry **IVORY** **TOGO** Benue River **AFRICAN REPUBLIC**
Freetown **COAST** **GHANA** Porto Novo Bangui Juba
SIERRA LEONE Yamoussoukro Lome Lagos Douala **UGANDA**
Monrovia Abidjan Accra **CAMEROON** (Zaire River) L. Albert **KENYA**
LIBERIA Yaounde Kisangani Kampala Mogadishu
EQUAT. Bata L. Victoria Nairobi
GUINEA Malabo **CONGO** **ZAIRE** **RWANDA** L. Victoria
Libreville **GABON** Kigali Mombasa
Brazzaville **BURUNDI** Bujumbura **TANZANIA**
Pointe-Noire Kinshasa Kalemie Dodoma
CABINDA Kananga Dar es Salaam

Indian Ocean

South Atlantic

Luanda L.Tanganyika Mbeya
Kasama
Lubumbashi
Lobito Luena **MALAWI**
ANGOLA Kitwe L. Nyasa Nacala
Namibe **ZAMBIA** Lilongwe
Lusaka
L. Kariba Harare
Walvis Bay Windhoek **ZIMBABWE** **MOZAMBIQUE**
NAMIBIA Bulawayo Mahajanga
Gaborone Antananarivo
BOTSWANA **MADAGASCAR**
Luderitz Pretoria Maputo
Johannesburg **SWAZILAND** Toliara
Maseru Mbabane
LESOTHO Durban
SOUTH AFRICA
Cape Port
Town Elizabeth

Africa

✪ National Capital
Bonn • City
--- National Boundary
— Rivers

0   Miles   100

The Heritage Library of African Peoples

SAMBURU

Jon Holtzman

THE ROSEN PUBLISHING GROUP, INC.
NEW YORK

Published in 1995 by The Rosen Publishing Group, Inc.
29 East 21st Street, New York, NY 10010

First Edition

Manufactured in the United States of America

Library of Congress Cataloging-in-Publication Data

Holtzman, Jon.
    Samburu / Jon Holtzman. — 1st ed.
      p. cm. — (The Heritage library of African peoples)
    Includes bibliographical references and index.
    ISBN 0-8239-1759-2
    1. Samburu (African people)—History—Juvenile literature.
    2. Samburu (African people)—Social life and customs—Juvenile
literature. I. Title. II. Series.
DT433.545.S26H65 1995
960'.04965—dc20   95-19655
                                                          CIP
                                                            AC

Contents

Introduction   6

1.   The People   9

2.   The Land   15

3.   Social Organization   22

4.   Religion and Rituals   32

5.   Daily Life   43

6.   The Colonial History of
     East Africa   50

7.   A View of the Future   55

     Glossary   60

     For Further Reading   61

     Index   62

INTRODUCTION

THERE IS EVERY REASON FOR US TO KNOW
something about Africa and to understand its
past and the way of life of its peoples. Africa is a
rich continent that has for centuries provided
the world with art, culture, labor, wealth, and
natural resources. It has vast mineral deposits,
fossil fuels, and commercial crops.

But perhaps most important is the fact that
fossil evidence indicates that human beings
originated in Africa. The earliest traces of
human beings and their tools are almost two
million years old. Their descendants have
migrated throughout the world. To be human is
to be of African descent.

The experiences of the peoples who stayed in
Africa are as rich and as diverse as of those who
established themselves elsewhere. This series of
books describes their environment, their modes
of subsistence, their relationships, and their
customs and beliefs. The books present the
variety of languages, histories, cultures, and
religions that are to be found on the African
continent. They demonstrate the historical link-
ages between African peoples and the way contemporary Africa has been affected by European
colonial rule.

Africa is large, complex, and diverse. It
encompasses an area of more than 11,700,000

square miles. The United States, Europe, and India could fit easily into it. The sheer size is an indication of the continent's great variety in geography, terrain, climate, flora, fauna, peoples, languages, and cultures.

Much of contemporary Africa has been shaped by European colonial rule, industrialization, urbanization, and the demands of a world economic system. For more than seventy years, large regions of Africa were ruled by Great Britain, France, Belgium, Portugal, and Spain. African peoples from various ethnic, linguistic, and cultural backgrounds were brought together to form colonial states.

For decades Africans struggled to gain their independence. It was not until after World War II that the colonial territories became independent African states. Today, almost all of Africa is ruled by Africans. Large numbers of Africans live in modern cities. Rural Africa is also being transformed, and yet its people still engage in many of their age-old customs and beliefs.

Contemporary circumstances and natural events have not always been kind to ordinary Africans. Today, however, new social movements and technological innovations pose great promise for future development.

George C. Bond
Institute of African Studies
Columbia University, New York City

The Samburu maintain a traditional culture even today.

chapter

1

THE PEOPLE

THE SAMBURU ARE A LIVESTOCK-HERDING tribe living in the arid plains and semideserts of northern Kenya. Their economy is based almost entirely on the raising of stock: cattle, goats, sheep, and sometimes camels. Like their better-known relatives the Maasai, the Samburu have until recently despised anyone who tills the soil and have refused to undertake any kind of agriculture.

Currently there are about 100,000 Samburu. They do not call themselves "Samburu"; that is a name their neighbors have given them. Rather, they call themselves Lokop or Loikop, which is possibly a reference to their status as "people of the land."

The Samburu maintain a traditional culture with a variety of unique social institutions. They

The Samburu call themselves Lokop or Loikop, which means "People of the Land."

and their ancestors have for centuries adapted to life in a harsh environment. In recent years, however, Western culture has affected the Samburu.

▼ ORIGINS OF THE SAMBURU ▼

The ancestors of the Samburu, and of other Maa-speaking peoples such as the Maasai and Lchamus, are believed to have migrated south through the Rift Valley centuries ago, aided by iron weapons and superior cattle that gave them an advantage over earlier inhabitants of the region. The people were probably organized into much smaller groups than the current ones, culturally similar but politically independent. The current peoples joined together, probably in alliances to aid in warfare.

The Samburu are believed to have broken off from the main Maasai migration around 1600. Their relationship is much closer to the Lchamus, with whom the Samburu lived in direct contact until around 1840. At that time the Samburu were driven northeast by the Turkana, while the Lchamus remained around Lake Baringo.

The Samburu themselves have no clearly defined beliefs about their origins. They say that they came from a place called Oto somewhere to the north. Oto is referred to when talking about the murky, indefinable past.

The Samburu belong to the Eastern Nilotic group of African peoples. The Nilotes are believed to have their origins in the Nile region of the Sudan and are one of the major linguistic-cultural groups in Africa. Other Nilotes include the Pokot, Turkana, Luo, and the Maasai, to whom the Samburu are closely related.

The Samburu speak a dialect of Maa, a language that they share with the Maasai and Lchamus of Kenya and the Arusha and

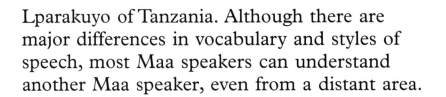

Lparakuyo of Tanzania. Although there are
major differences in vocabulary and styles of
speech, most Maa speakers can understand
another Maa speaker, even from a distant area.

▼ PHYSICAL APPEARANCE ▼

The physical features of the Samburu vary
widely. While their skin is generally dark, it can
range from a very dark brown to almost reddish.
The hair, while dark, has a wide range of tex-
tures, from kinky with very tight curls to almost
completely straight.

Much of this variation can be accounted for
by the common practice of intermarriage with
neighboring groups. The Turkana, who border
the Samburu to the north and west, are commonly very dark, with heavy features. The
Rendille and Boran, who live to the east, tend
to be somewhat lighter in complexion, with
straight or wavy hair.

The Samburu are generally quite slender in
stature. This may have some genetic basis, as a
slight build generally is an advantage in a hot,
dry environment. It is likely, however, that the
main causes are their often meager diet and the
demands of life in a difficult environment.

▼ STYLE OF DRESS ▼

The Samburu have a generally simple mode
of dress. Prior to the acquisition of cloth, they

Samburu ornamentation is elaborate and highly decorative.

Samburu warriors often paint their faces and wear elaborate hairdressings.

dressed in skins from cows or goats. Samburu women still wear a leather apron, but now usually cover it with a cloth. They also wear a cloth or two around their torso, but they sometimes go bare-breasted, especially around the home. Samburu men usually wear one or two cloths or blankets, wrapped around the waist or over the shoulder like a toga.

While the clothes are simple, Samburu ornamentation is elaborate and highly decorative. The main feature is colorful beadwork worn as necklaces, bracelets, and earrings. Children often wear a string or two of beads even before they wear clothes. Some styles of beadwork are traditional for at least a few generations; others are modern imitations of Western objects such as bow ties or crosses. Most ornaments are worn simply for personal enhancement, but others show the status of the wearer or are believed to have supernatural powers.▲

chapter

2

THE LAND

THE SAMBURU LIVE IN NORTHERN KENYA,
almost directly on the equator. Most live in
Samburu District. The Samburu have moved
generally southward in recent years, and some
now live in neighboring Isiolo and Laikipia Dis-
tricts. Isolated communities of Samburu continue to live to the north on Mount Marsabit
and Mount Kulal, which were once within the
Samburu homelands.

▼ CLIMATE AND TOPOGRAPHY ▼

The lands of the Samburu are generally quite
dry. Rainfall is unreliable and often inadequate.
Temperatures are very hot in some areas and
moderate in others, but they usually range
between 70 and 90 degrees F.

The land is divided into highlands and
lowlands. Along the equator, the higher areas
are cooler and receive more rainfall than lower

areas. Some parts of Kenya are so dry and hot
that almost no creature can live; other parts are
lush and fertile.

The principal highland area is the Leroghi
Plateau, known to the Samburu as Ldonyo,
"the Mountain." On the plateau, temperatures range in the 70s to 80s. Rainfall is not
high, but streams or springs provide a permanent source of water in most areas. The land is
mostly open grassland or bush, with forest in the

The arid lands on which the Samburu live often necessitate the digging of wells.

highest areas. Agriculture is possible in some areas.

The lowlands, which make up most of the land, are much drier, hotter, and harsher. Temperatures are often in the high 90s, and even in the best of times there are months without rain. During droughts in some areas it may not rain for years. The lowlands have little grass, and most of the vegetation is acacia thorn trees. Permanent water sources are few, and people usually must rely on wells dug in dry river beds.

▼ THE ENVIRONMENT AND ▼
THE WAY OF LIFE

Pastoralism, the raising of livestock, is the only possible means of survival in most of the

The Samburu rely on herds of cattle, goats, and sheep to survive in their dry environment.

area. Lacking enough rain to raise crops, the Samburu must rely on their herds of cattle, goats, sheep, and in some cases, camels.

Environmental factors also often require a nomadic lifestyle. In semidesert areas livestock may quickly eat all the available grass and browse, and the Samburu then need to move the herds to new pastures. The rain that does fall may be restricted to very small areas. With news of rain in a particular area, people often migrate to take advantage of it.

▼ NOMADISM ▼

Nomadism is divided into two main types, *true nomadism* and *transhumance*. In true nomadism, entire families move along with their animals on a regular basis. Such a migration is sometimes temporary or seasonal, but it is also possible that a family may never return to the place they have left.

In *transhumance* the animals are divided into two groups. Some are taken by herders to better pastures, and some remain behind. The migration is seasonal. The herders search for areas where the rains have been good, and they return with the animals when it has rained at home.

The degree of nomadism is highest in the driest areas, where the pasture is less rich and more dispersed. True nomadism is still typical in the lowlands but rare in the highlands, where transhumance is commonly practiced.

▼ SAMBURU SETTLEMENTS ▼

The Samburu typically live in small settlements surrounded by a fence of acacia thorns. Settlements usually consist of three to five families, but single-family settlements are common.

Each family has its own gate to the settlement, and each married woman has her own house. The Samburu are polygynous, meaning that a man may have more than one wife. Each wife builds her own house out of cow dung plastered onto a wooden frame. Men sleep in the houses of their wives.

These huts are examples of traditional Samburu huts made of cow dung plastered onto wooden frames.

The Samburu and Wildlife

The lands of the Samburu are home to many species of wild animals: elephants, lions, zebras, crocodiles, and many others.

Traditionally, the Samburu rarely hunted. Hunters were *dorobo*, poor people who had no cattle. In times of great hunger, some animals such as buffalo and eland (a large antelope) were hunted. Other animals, however, were never eaten. The Samburu believe, for instance, that elephants resemble humans, and eating them is completely forbidden. Even people who have hunted elephants for ivory are despised for having "eaten an elephant."

The Samburu National Reserve is an important sanctuary for many species of animals. Every year it is visited by thousands of tourists from all over the world. Tourism such as this is the most important source of income for Kenya. Unfortunately, most of the profits go to hotels and tour companies, rather than African peoples such as the Samburu who sacrificed land for the reserve.

Although the settlements are not clustered together to form true villages, it is common for them to be grouped into neighborhoods. Having neighbors nearby helps to provide safety. Usually at least a few settlements are visible to one another, some perhaps being within shouting distance.▲

chapter

3

SOCIAL ORGANIZATION

AGE IS THE GUIDING PRINCIPLE OF SAMBURU social organization. A person's age and gender are the most important factors in shaping his or her role in society. Age defines all aspects of a Samburu's life: the work you do, how you must greet someone, when and whom you may marry, and even what you may eat. Samburu males and females of every age must follow precise rules of behavior.

▼ AGE-SETS ▼

Samburu men are grouped into age-sets. Men of an age-set are initiated into manhood during the same period in an elaborate ceremony focused on circumcision. Those men will be comrades throughout life. Youths are initiated at ages ranging from about fourteen to twenty, and initiations for a single age group continue

After a Samburu boy is circumcised, he must wear a black skin and ostrich feathers until he is ready to enter the next stage toward adulthood.

The *murran* are regarded as very glamorous.

over a period of many years. Usually, about fourteen years elapse between the beginning of one age-set and the beginning of inititiations for the next. Men of the same age-set may be separated by fifteen or more years but are treated as being the same age.

▼ THE *MURRAN* ▼

Each age-set has a different role in society. The most recently circumcised group are the *murran*, commonly referred to as warriors. The *murran* are responsible for the most difficult and dangerous tasks. Traditionally, warfare was one of their most important roles. Although some small-scale cattle raiding still goes on, work such as taking animals long distances for pasture during the dry season is much more important today.

The *murran* are expected to live at the edge of Samburu society. They are not allowed to marry or to eat any food that has been seen by an initiated woman. Ideally they spend their time away from settlements, in the bush, eating meat with their age-mates. Despite these restrictions, the *murran* are regarded as very glamorous, and they spend a lot of time making themselves attractive. The most striking feature of their appearance is their hair, which they wear in long braids, covered with red ochre. They practice singing and dancing, which are important skills in their attempts to win girlfriends.

▼ THE ELDERS ▼

Each age-set remains *murran* for about fourteen years, until the circumcision of the next age-set. With the initiation of a new group of *murran*, they shave off their long red braids, marry, and settle into the life of elderhood.

Elders are those who wield the most power in Samburu society. Although all elders are

Elders wield the most power in Samburu society.

Samburu women are usually married in their early to mid-teen years.

supposed to be equal, older age-sets always command greater respect. The youngest age-set of elders are usually the most active and are responsible for organizing meetings, ceremonies, and other activities.

Elders two groups ahead of the *murran* are called *lpiroi*, or firestick elders. They are the sponsors of the *murran* and responsible for advising them. They also discipline the *murran* through fines and cursing when it is deemed necessary.

As he ages, an elder gradually becomes less active in society. He participates less and less in meetings and gives his sons primary responsibility for the care of his herds. Eventually he distributes his property to his sons and lives out the remainder of his years as a dependent in the home of his eldest son.

▼ WOMEN ▼

The organization of women is not nearly as precisely defined as is that of men. They do not have organized age groups, but age is still an important factor in determining their status. They are usually married in their early to middle teenage years and are at least fifteen years younger than their husband. A woman's status is at first low, as a junior member in her new husband's unfamiliar home. Gradually her status rises as she ages and bears children. She really gains stature when her sons start to become *murran*.

Descent is patrilineal among the Samburu. Names and property are passed only from fathers to sons. All Samburu names begin with

A Samburu warrior or *murran*.

the prefix *Le-*, *Lo-*, or *La-*, such as Leleruk,
Loloju, or Lanyasunya. This prefix means "of"
and identifies the person's father. At death, or
earlier if a man lives to be old, a man's livestock
is divided among his sons. His daughters cannot
inherit.

Women take the identity of their husband's
family after marriage. Although she cannot
inherit property from her father, a young woman
may have received livestock as a gift, and she
brings it to the marriage. Nevertheless, most if
not all livestock is regarded as belonging to the
husband in Samburu families.

A short while after marriage, a girl returns to
the family of her birth, where her mother gives
her all the household items she will need. These
include calabashes in which milk is stored, pots
and other household utensils, and *sainia*, a
kind of rack used to load goods on donkeys
while migrating. These forms of property, along
with the house, belong exclusively to the
woman.

▼ SECTIONS ▼

Families that are believed to be related are
grouped together into *lmarei*, or sections. All
people in the section are said to be related to a
mythical ancestor, although no one can trace the
actual relationships. The Samburu are divided
into a total of eight sections. Members of the

same section cannot marry because of the supposed relationships.

The only exception to the rule against marrying within the section is the Lmasula, which is the largest of the Samburu sections. The Lmasula section is said to be "like the dung of the elephant" because it is so big, including many clans and subclans. As a consequence, Lmasula members are allowed to marry.

Samburu sections are not territorial units, but people of the same section often like to live in the same area. Age-set ceremonies are also organized on the basis of section. Thus, people of the same section come together at ritual occasions and are often slow to disperse. Today, sections are not important as political units, but they still play an important role in regulating marriage and ritual life.▲

chapter

4

RELIGION AND RITUALS

THE SAMBURU BELIEVE THAT SUPERNATURAL forces are active players in everyday life. Almost anything that happens—death, accident, unusual weather, or good or bad fortune with herds—may be attributed to supernatural causes. Perhaps a person who suffers an untimely death had been cursed by his uncle, or perhaps he had committed some grave offense against the Samburu sense of right and wrong. A person whose herds are thriving may have had a lucky goat born in his herd, or perhaps he has stolen the luck of a now less fortunate neighbor. Or possibly the ultimate explanation lies simply in the work of the deity.

The Samburu are monotheistic, believing in a single deity, Nkai. The Samburu associate the deity closely with the sky, and rain, and Nkai is believed to be the creative force behind all things.

WAYS OF STUDYING THE PAST

Studying the past of groups like the Samburu poses special problems. The Samburu traditionally had no writing, and few Europeans visited them before the twentieth century. In addition, even the records left by early explorers provide little useful information. Scholars today must try to piece together a picture of the past through a variety of methods.

One of the most important tools they use is comparative linguistics. Comparative linguistics examines the similarities and differences between languages. This information can reveal how the speakers of these languages may have been related in the past.

Cultures such as the Samburu often hand down through the generations the stories of important events. Through a careful study of this "oral history," one can often separate what really happened from distortions that have occurred in the stories. Archeological excavations can also reveal how people lived in the past, and even which groups were living where at a particular time.

Prayers are a feature of everyday life. Virtually all gatherings are blessed with a series of elaborate prayers spoken by the elders. Elders also pray in their settlements every morning. Often women pray among their cows while milking.

▼ RITUALS ▼

The most important Samburu rituals concern life transitions such as birth, initiation, marriage, and death. Important in most cultures, these transitions are of particular significance to the Samburu, who put such a strong emphasis on dividing the society into age groups. People's age is defined not so much by their years of life as by their "social age." To the Samburu, this is mainly defined by the rites of passages they have undergone. A fourteen-year-old *murran* is considered to be senior to an eighteen-year-old youth who has not been circumcised and could even punish him as if he were a child.

Other rituals are performed to help individuals or families, such as to help women conceive children, to bless families, or to remove curses.

▼ CIRCUMCISION AND AGE-SET RITUALS ▼

For Samburu men, the age-set rituals are the most important events of their lives. At circumcision and the rituals that follow it, a boy moves into manhood. He becomes a member of an age-set that will be his peer group throughout life.

A new age-set is formed approximately every fourteen years. Circumcisions begin with the Lmasula section on the sacred Mount Ng'iro to the north. Other sections then gather in large settlements called *lorrora*, and boys go about collecting things that will be needed in the ritual: the gum of special trees, and water from a permanent water source. In most families, boys

This boy has just entered the transitional period following initiation.

are circumcised at dawn, after staying up all night singing special songs with men of the community. As soon as there is enough sunlight so that the operation can be performed with precision, the boy is stripped of a special black skin he has been wearing for the occasion, held steady by two sponsors, and circumcised.

Samburu circumcisions are wild, emotional occasions. Overcome with the importance of the ceremony, and with sympathy for the boy, many people fall into a form of violent trance. Their friends must physically restrain them to prevent them from hurting themselves. People have been known to crash through thorn fences and hurtle head first into boulders.

These *murran* are about to become *Ipayan*, or married men.

Following the circumcision, initiates enter a special transitional period. During this time the initiate eats special foods, sleeps on a special bed, and spends his days hunting birds, which he then wears on his head. After about a month a ceremony is performed in which the boy discards the birds and becomes a full *murran*. From this time he must follow the prohibitions of the *murran* and may no longer eat in his mother's house.

▼ MARRIAGE AND *LMINONG* ▼

Marriage brings important changes in the status of both men and women. Men move into elderhood and assume the responsibilities of managing a family and household. Through marriage girls become women. Frequently a girl's wedding occurs on the day of the initiation.

A man needs to get the girl's family's permission to marry, and there are long negotiations over the amount of bridewealth that he will pay. Usually the groom gives the girl's family five to seven cattle and one or two sheep, each animal having a particular symbolic and social purpose. The payment of a cash sum and other gifts is typical, though not obligatory.

The ceremony takes place over three days at the settlement of the girl's family. On the first day the groom arrives in the evening, with a party of a dozen or more male friends and relatives who will assist him in the marriage. The bridewealth animals are brought, and there may be some singing and dancing.

At dawn the next day the groom and his party slaughter the marriage ox outside the door of the house where the girl is staying. The slaughter of the ox is the act that actually forges the marriage; it is sometimes compared to "the marriage certificate." Blessings are performed, tobacco is distributed, the meat is eaten, and tea is drunk. In the afternoon there is dancing, and the bride may come out of the house in which she had been staying all day. She makes her first appearance as a married woman and says goodbye to her friends and her life of

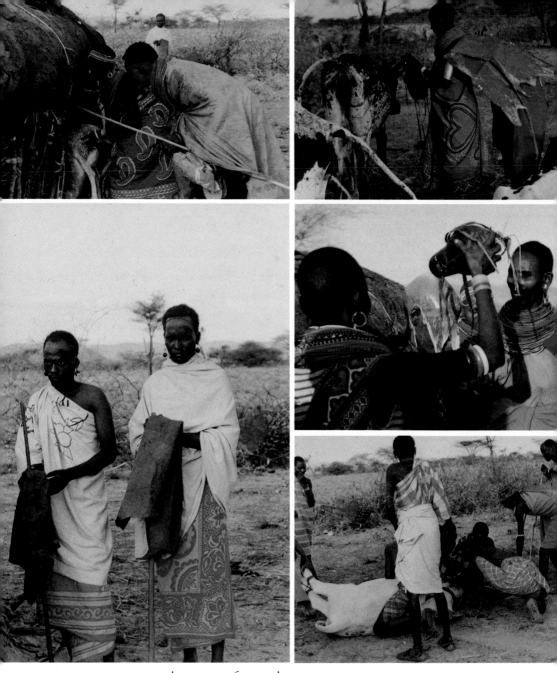

Ritual aspects of a Samburu marriage ceremony.

childhood. The bride and groom may be
up most of the night, being lectured by the
elders on how they should behave as married
people.

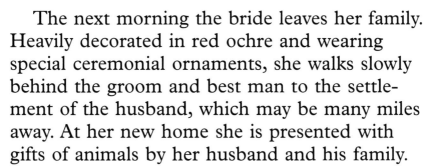

The next morning the bride leaves her family. Heavily decorated in red ochre and wearing special ceremonial ornaments, she walks slowly behind the groom and best man to the settlement of the husband, which may be many miles away. At her new home she is presented with gifts of animals by her husband and his family.

Marriage does not automatically remove the prohibitions that a man has as a *murran*. These are removed in the *lminong* ceremony, which usually occurs a few months after marriage. This ceremony lifts the restrictions against a man's eating food that has been seen by women, and he may now eat food prepared for him by his wife. Also during this ceremony, the women welcome the new wife to the area.

▼ FERTILITY RITUALS ▼

Bearing children is central to women's role in Samburu society. To lead a happy and normal life, it is essential that a woman have children, and if she fails to give birth, rituals are performed to assist her.

The *Ndorosi* may be performed after some bad event suggests that Nkai might be angry and women's fertility could thus be threatened. Women march about the countryside in large groups, singing and blessing. They may go to particular settlements, demanding animals for the ceremony. They also select socially accept-

Bearing children is essential to women's role in Samburu society.

able sexual partners for women whose husbands have failed to give them children. The men selected are of proven potency and cannot refuse to comply. At the end of this frenzied period, a blessing is performed by the elders.

A ritual performed for an individual woman who has had trouble having children is known as *Remore*. It is performed by uncircumcised boys who dress like *murran*. They dance for the woman and bless her by presenting her with a figurine representing the child. The woman should then give birth to a child of the sex selected by the boys.

▼ DEATH ▼

Death rituals depend heavily on the status of

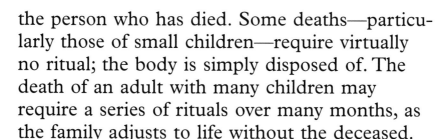

the person who has died. Some deaths—particularly those of small children—require virtually no ritual; the body is simply disposed of. The death of an adult with many children may require a series of rituals over many months, as the family adjusts to life without the deceased.

The Samburu tend to make a distinction between timely and untimely deaths. The death of *murran*, older children, and adults who have no children are considered to be untimely and must not occur in the home. Such people are removed from the home immediately before death in order to avoid occurrence of an offense. The death of an old person is considered normal. Children should gather for the death of an old man, and his oldest son should be there to hold his head and hear his final words. The death of the elder usually means the dispersal of the family, and all his sons should be present for the rituals following his death.

It is considered wrong to say the name of a dead person, because hearing the name will remind people of him or her and make them sad. A person may change his or her name if it is the same as that of someone who has died.

The Samburu do not have strongly developed beliefs about the afterlife. Generally they believe that when people die they are simply dead. There is some vague idea, however, that people may continue to exist after death.

THE CURSE

The Samburu hold a strong belief in the ability to lay a curse. Most misfortune—especially unusual or accidental death—is thought to be caused by a curse.

The most potent curse is against one's own relatives. Usually it is older people who curse younger ones, and the threat of a curse is an important method of control.

Certain families called *laisi* are believed to have a powerful curse and also an ability to foretell the future. People are afraid to offend *laisi* and don't like to marry into some *laisi* families. Other families are believed to "own" certain things, like elephants, fire, or snakes. They can make themselves immune from these things, while using them against others.

Laibons are a special group of diviners. Samburu *laibons* are not as important as those of the Maasai, who were political leaders. They are important, however, in identifying and correcting the supernatural causes behind a person's problems. People may go to a *laibon* if something bad has happened, and he will tell them what to do to overcome the problem. The *laibon* may also predict future events or assist in inflicting supernatural harm against someone else. Samburu often go to Maasai *laibons* for these purposes, as they are thought to be more powerful.

Traditionally the Samburu did not bury their dead. The body was simply smeared with fat, covered with leaves, and left in the bush to be eaten by hyenas. The only exception was old and respected men, with many children, who could be buried in the middle of their settlement. Today, because of pressure from the government and Christian missions, many Samburu now bury their dead.▲

42

5

DAILY LIFE

THE DAILY LIFE OF THE SAMBURU IS CENTERED around the care of the animals. The herds must be taken out to graze every single day.

People rise before dawn to begin the day's work. Children take the animals out to graze. Women relight the fire and make the tea and porridge, which will be the only meal for most people until evening. The women also milk the animals and open the gates of the settlement.

The workday ends around dusk when the animals are brought home and milked. For the rest of the evening people relax around the home, talking, telling stories, or sometimes singing. Usually they go to bed early to prepare for the next day's work.

▼ WORK ▼

Like most things in Samburu society, work is divided to a great extent by age and gender.

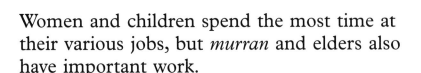

Women and children spend the most time at their various jobs, but *murran* and elders also have important work.

Children are the most important herders on a day-to-day basis. At the age of six or seven they begin herding sheep and goats near the home. The herder must have the skill and knowledge to direct the animals to the best places to graze. He or she also must keep track of all the animals and risks severe punishment if any do not return home safely.

Murran are usually responsible for the most difficult herding. They take animals to cattle camps during the dry season, often trekking long distances. Older boys and girls often accompany *murran* to the cattle camps. *Murran* are also often responsible for the buying and selling of animals. This can be a dangerous job. Sometimes they have to travel sixty to eighty miles on foot through areas frequented by bandits to reach the livestock markets.

Women's work is perhaps the most strenuous, as they are responsible for collecting water and firewood. Sometimes they use donkeys, but at other times they walk several miles with heavy loads slung over their backs. Besides this, they cook, milk animals, watch children, and make and repair houses and household utensils. It is also common for women—especially younger wives—to do some herding, especially of goats.

The work of men varies a great deal. The
cultural ideal is that men should be managers,
planning work and directing others in their
tasks. Some men, in fact, do very little work and
prefer to sit around talking with other elders.
Other men are quite industrious and perform
vital tasks. Younger elders often continue to
do the work they did when they were *murran*.
Some elders are forced to herd if there are not
enough children; others choose to do the herding because they enjoy it. It is also the responsibility of men to water the animals, which in very
dry areas is one of the most difficult jobs in
Samburu life. A man may have to stand in a
well six feet deep or more, scooping water into a
trough with a small bucket.

The most popular forms of recreation are
singing and dancing. All special occasions are
celebrated with singing and dancing, and children and *murran* often dance simply for pleas-
ure. *Murran* are the most spectacular dancers,
often leaping high in the air. Except for small
children and very old people, everyone participates in dances. They are an occasion for everyone to look their best, wearing their best clothes
and decorating themselves with red ochre and
beads.

For old men, a board game called *intotoi* fills
much leisure time. A variation of the *mbao* game
that is popular throughout East Africa, it con-

Dances are occasions for everyone to look their best. They wear their best clothes and beads. The *murran* decorate themselves with red ochre.

sists of a simple board with two rows of holes. Each player moves stones along his side and tries to capture all the stones from the opponent's side. The game is a metaphor for pastoral life, as the stones represent cattle. When you capture stones you have eaten your opponent's cattle, and after six victories you have eaten his house.

▼ MEALS ▼

The traditional diet of the Samburu was based only on the products of their animals: milk, meat, and blood. Although they always had access to other foods—such as honey from hunters in the forest, or grain from agricultural neighbors—being able to survive only on their herds has always been an important goal for the Samburu.

Milk is the staple of the diet. It can be drunk fresh or allowed to ferment for several days until it is similar to yoghurt or cottage cheese. Milk is stored in calabashes that are cleaned with burning sticks, giving it a smoky flavor. Milk is stored in separate calabashes. A large one for the elder is called *natuu*. If a family has *murran* there is a separate calabash for them.

Meat is not eaten as frequently as milk. Cows are rarely slaughtered simply for food. Usually they are slaughtered only on ritual occasions, although the Samburu also eat any animal that has died. Sheep and goats are sometimes slaughtered for food, especially for visitors. Many rules govern the distribution of meat. Elders, *murran*, women, and boys and girls all are entitled to a particular share. Certain parts of animals must not be eaten by the owner, but must be given away to friends or neighbors.

Blood is the least commonly eaten food. It is primarily a food for the dry season, when milk may not be available, and for *murran* at cattle camps. A small arrow is shot into a cow's neck, and the wound is sealed when enough blood has been collected. Blood may be drunk plain,

A young warrior sucks blood from the jugular vein of a recently sacrificed bull.

A warrior divides the meat of the sacrificed bull.

The meat is blessed by the elders by means of a sacred tree.

mixed with milk, or cooked into porridge with wild greens. Blood is also drunk fresh from the neck of animals when they are slaughtered.

Murran have special rules concerning their food. They may not eat food that has been seen by women, except for milk, which they may drink if they are in the company of another *murran*. Ideally they should be eating meat in the bush with their age-mates, and they may be given animals for that purpose, or try to capture some through raids or theft.

Other foods have been introduced to the Samburu in recent decades and are now important to their diet, particularly maize meal and tea. Maize meal is eaten as a thick porridge. It is eaten plain, or mixed with milk or fat. Tea is both a staple food and a food of hospitality for visitors to the home. Usually it is prepared with a lot of milk and sugar. When it was first introduced around the 1940s, it was reserved primarily for old men. As drought and disease reduced the amount of available milk, people found they could stretch it by making it into tea.▲

6
THE COLONIAL HISTORY
OF EAST AFRICA

EUROPEANS FIRST CAME TO THE LANDS OF THE
Samburu in the late nineteenth century. For
the most part they were British and Germans,
who came both to explore and to establish
claims for their countries. These early explorers
were guided by Arab and Swahili traders from
the East African coast. The traders were already
familiar with the area, having made expeditions
into the interior for some time in search of ivory
and slaves.

East Africa eventually came to be divided
between the British and the Germans. The
Germans established a claim to the area that is
now Tanzania, while the British occupied Kenya
and Uganda. Following World War I, British rule
was established throughout East Africa. Sub-
jugation of the peoples of East Africa began in
the 1890s. Their land was coveted, and their
labor was exploited to aid European development.

The peoples living in the most fertile areas or near European farms and towns suffered the most, losing much of their best land and being subjected to forced labor. The Samburu were affected much less, as most of their land held little interest for European settlers. Nevertheless, they lost their independence and were forced to undergo many changes.

▼ BRITISH COLONIAL RULE ▼

British officers were sent to Samburu lands near the beginning of the twentieth century. Little military force was needed to subdue the Samburu, who were severely weakened after the disaster of the 1890s. A six-year drought combined with epidemic cattle disease had decimated their herds, so that many Samburu had to survive by hunting wild animals or seeking refuge with other tribes. To make matters worse, a smallpox epidemic had killed many people, especially the young and strong. The Samburu were in no position to resist the British and actually found them to be powerful allies against their archenemies, the Turkana.

The first permanent British station was established in Samburu District at Barsaloi in 1924. The district headquarters was moved to the cooler, more hospitable climate of the Leroghi Plateau when Maralal was founded in 1934. The British ruled the Samburu both directly and

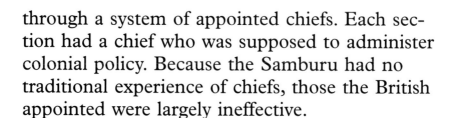

through a system of appointed chiefs. Each section had a chief who was supposed to administer colonial policy. Because the Samburu had no traditional experience of chiefs, those the British appointed were largely ineffective.

▼ COLONIAL POLICY ▼

The British were not particularly active in trying to promote change and development in Samburu District. The district had little economic potential, nor was it near areas that did. It was made a "closed district," and travel in and out was severely restricted, particularly for Africans. The British were mainly interested in maintaining peace and in reorganizing aspects of the pastoral economy that they considered destructive to the environment.

The *murran* were perceived as a group of idle, dangerous young men and the main threat to peace in the district. In the eyes of the British, the *murran* did little productive work and were encouraged to prove their bravery by stealing cattle and killing enemies.

The British took great pains to destroy the institution of *murranhood. Murran* were forced to do jobs such as building roads and dams and doing locust control. Spears were often banned, and the British tried to force the *murran* to marry early in the hope that the responsibilities of elderhood would cool their high spirits. The *murran* refused to be repressed. Most *murran* enjoyed their lifestyle and were not prepared to marry. As the policing of Samburu District became more repressive, however, and the fact of punishment more clear, traditional *murran* practices decreased.

Uncontrolled overgrazing by the herds of the Samburu was also seen as a major problem by the British. The use of certain pastureland was severely restricted, and violators were arrested and their cattle seized. The Samburu had their own methods of

The British took great pains to destroy the institution of *murranhood*.

preventing overgrazing and strongly disliked those imposed by the British. They understood their environment much better than the British newcomers and saw most of the grazing restrictions as unnecessary and even harmful.

Other aspects of change did not occur rapidly

in the colonial period. Most Samburu still had large herds and were not interested in changing their way of life. Nor were the British much interested in promoting widespread change. A Christian mission and school opened near Maralal in the 1930s, but it had little impact in the colonial period. The Samburu showed little initial interest in seeking employment, although by the 1940s *murran* were beginning to enlist in the army and police. A number of Samburu fought in Burma in World War II and were said to have served with exceptional bravery.

▼ THE END OF COLONIAL RULE ▼

Kenya gained its independence from the British in 1964. While this had a tremendous impact on many of the fertile, densely populated regions of the country, its effects on Samburu District were not profound. There is little Samburu representation in the government, and many still see it as a body somewhat foreign to their way of life.

The Kenyan government has, however, taken a somewhat more active role in promoting development in the district, particularly in education. With the end of colonial rule, movement in and out of the district was no longer restricted, and many more Samburu began traveling to Nairobi and other parts of Kenya in search of work.▲

chapter

7

A VIEW OF THE FUTURE

THE RATE OF CHANGE AMONG THE SAMBURU has increased rapidly in recent years. While most Samburu remain traditional in many ways, and almost all maintain a respect for Samburu culture, challenges lie ahead for the Samburu in the coming years.

The greatest threat to the Samburu and their way of life is the severe decline in their pastoral economy. In recent years a series of severe droughts, disease epidemics, and changes in herding practices have caused a severe decline in the size of the herds. At the same time, rapid population growth has strained the economy. As a consequence increasing numbers of Samburu—especially *murran*—have gone to big towns to look for jobs. Many Samburu in the most fertile areas have planted small farms to supplement their income.

Samburu culture has remained traditional in many ways. Even most Samburu who have lived outside the district for many years take pride in being Samburu and always return home for important occasions such as the initiation of a new age-set.

Nevertheless, powerful forces are propelling change. As young men leave in large numbers to seek employment, they experience many new things, bringing into question the value of some aspects of Samburu life.

Western education has also become popular in recent years. Most Samburu want to send at least some of their children to school. Education is seen as a means for them to get employment, which will help to support the whole family. Children in boarding school do not learn about traditional culture.

Christian missionaries are also very active in Samburu district. It is hard to know the extent to which Christianity has had an impact on Samburu beliefs, but the missions have had a major economic impact, providing jobs, relief food, and health care and sponsoring many schools and students.

▼ OUTLOOK FOR THE SAMBURU ▼

The future of the Samburu is uncertain. It is crucial that they recover economically if they are to prosper and their culture to remain strong.

Despite the powerful forces of modernity, most Samburu who have lived outside the district for many years take pride in being Samburu and always return home for important occasions such as the initiation of a new age-set. These young men perform traditional Samburu dances.

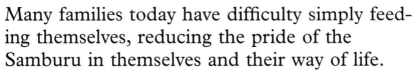

Many families today have difficulty simply feeding themselves, reducing the pride of the Samburu in themselves and their way of life.

A number of possibilities hold promise for improving the future prospects of the Samburu. Improved veterinary services could reduce the number of animals lost to disease. An increased reliance on camels could also yield benefits, as camels are more resistant than cattle to drought and disease. Game ranching may also allow Samburu to raise native species that are better adapted to the harsh environment of Samburu District. Some would like to see family planning instituted, but it is not compatible with traditional culture.

The outlook for Samburu culture is much better. Few Samburu would like to see their valued traditions disappear. The vast majority still undergo traditional life rituals such as initiation and marriage. Not everyone follows the rules of the age-set system strictly, but the values are maintained as an essential part of Samburu life.

The Samburu have always been a dynamic people adapting themselves to a difficult environment. They are changing, but in ways that are consistent with their own values and beliefs. Just as they have always adapted themselves, they are adapting to a different life in a different time.▲

This store in Nairobi is one example of the way in which the Samburu have adapted to the modern world. Many Samburu no longer make the cloth in which they traditionally clothe themselves; they buy the cloth here. Note the paintings of Samburu people on either side of the doorway.

Glossary

dorobo Poor people who have to hunt animals to live.

intoitoi Board game popular with the elders.

laibon Diviners.

laisi Families believed to have particularly strong powers to curse.

lorrora Settlement in which circumcision is performed.

lpiroi Clan of aged elders.

mission Ministry sent by a church to convert nonbelievers.

myth Traditional story to explain a belief or practice.

nomadism Practice of traveling from place to place seasonally to find food.

oral history Stories passed down from parents to children to preserve the great events of the family.

pastoralism Livestock-raising as a way of life.

patrilinear Descent through the male line.

transhumance Form of nomadism in which families do not migrate, but send herders with cattle to find places to graze.

For Further Reading

Berg-Schlosser, Dirk. *Tradition and Change in Kenya*. Munich: Ferdinand Schoning, 1984.

Fedders, Andre, and Salvatori, Cynthia. *Peoples and Cultures of Kenya*. Nairobi: TransAfrica, 1979.

Lamb, David. *The Africans*. New York: Random House, 1987.

Ogot, Bethwell A. *Historical Dictionary of Kenya*. Metuchen, NJ, and London: The Scarecrow Press, Inc., 1981.

Oliver, Roland. *The African Experience*. New York: HarperCollins, 1991.

Pavitt, Nigel. *Samburu*. New York: Henry Holt & Co, 1992.

Index

A
age-sets, 22–25, 58
agriculture, 9, 17
appearance, physical, 12
Arusha, 11

B
blood, as food, 47–48
bridewealth, 37
British colonial rule, 51–54
burial, 42

C
camels, 9, 18, 58
cattle, 9, 18, 37

Christianity, 54, 56
circumcision, 22, 34–36
climate, 15–17
curse, 28, 32, 42

D
death rituals, 40–41
descent, patrilineal, 28–30
disease epidemics, 49, 51, 55
dress, style of, 12–14
drought, 17, 49, 51, 55

E
education, Western, 56
elders, 25–28, 47

environment, harsh, 10,
17–18

F
family planning, 58

G
game ranching, 58
goats, 9, 18, 47

H
herding, 19, 44, 55

I
initiation, 34–36, 58
ipayan (married men), 36

L
laibon (diviner), 42
laisi (family with strong
curse), 42
language
Maa, 10, 11
Nilotic, 11
Lchamus, 10–11
Ldonyo ("the Mountain"),
16
lmarei (sections), 30–31, 34,
52
Lmasula section, 31, 34
lminong (husbands'
ceremony), 36, 39
Lokop (Loikop), "people of
the land," 9
lorrora (settlements), 34
Lparakuo, 12

lpiroi (elders), 28

M
Maasai, 9, 10, 11
maize meal, 49
marriage, 36–39, 58
meals, 46–49
meat, 47
milk, as diet staple, 47
murran (warriors), 24–25,
28, 44–45, 47, 49, 55
British campaign against,
52–53

N
Ndorosi (fertility rituals),
39–40
Ng'iro (sacred mount), 34
Nkai (deity), 32, 39
nomadism, 18–19

O
ornamentation, 14
Oto (mythic origin), 11
overgrazing, 53–54

P
pastoralism, 9, 17–18, 55
polygyny, 19
prayer, 33

R
rainfall, 15–16
recreation, 45–46
Remore (fertility ritual), 40
rituals, 33–42

S
sanctuary, animal, 21
settlements, 17–21
sheep, 9, 18, 37, 47
supernaturalism, 32

T
temperature, 15

topography, 15–17
transhumance, 18–19

W
wildlife, 21
women's role, 28–30, 44, 47
work, division of, 43–45

ABOUT THE AUTHOR
Jon Holtzman received a bachelor's degree in anthropology from Haverford College, and a master's degree in anthropology from the University of Michigan. He is currently conducting doctoral research on aspects of social and economic change among the Samburu people of northern Kenya.

PHOTO CREDITS: p. 59 © Jon Holtzman; all other photos © CFM, Nairobi
DESIGN: Kim Sonsky
PHOTO RESEARCH: Vera Ahmadzadeh with Jennifer Croft